Discovering
South
America

COLOMBIA

Discovering
South
America

COLOMBIA

LeeAnne Gelletly

Mason Crest Publishers
Philadelphia

Produced by OTTN Publishing, Stockton, N.J.

Mason Crest Publishers
370 Reed Road
Broomall, PA 19008
www.masoncrest.com

3 5 7 9 8 6 4 2

Library of Congress Cataloging-in-Publication Data

Gelletly, LeeAnne.
  Colombia / LeeAnne Gelletly.
      p. cm. — (Discovering South America)
Includes bibliographical references and index.
  ISBN 1-59084-292-8
1. Colombia—Juvenile literature. I. Title. II. Series.
F2258.5 .G45 2003
986.1—dc21

                                                    2002011897

Discovering
South
America

Argentina		Paraguay
Bolivia	**South America:**	Peru
Brazil	Facts & Figures	Suriname
Chile	Ecuador	Uruguay
Colombia	Guyana	Venezuela

Table of Contents

Discovering South America

James D. Henderson

South America is a cornucopia of natural resources, a treasure house of ecological variety. It is also a continent of striking human diversity and geographic extremes. Yet in spite of that, most South Americans share a set of cultural similarities. Most of the continent's inhabitants are properly termed "Latin" Americans. This means that they speak a Romance language (one closely related to Latin), particularly Spanish or Portuguese. It means, too, that most practice Roman Catholicism and share the Mediterranean cultural patterns brought by the Spanish and Portuguese who settled the continent over five centuries ago.

Still, it is never hard to spot departures from these cultural norms. Bolivia, Peru, and Ecuador, for example, have significant Indian populations who speak their own languages and follow their own customs. In Paraguay the main Indian language, Guaraní, is accepted as official along with Spanish. Nor are all South Americans Catholics. Today Protestantism is making steady gains, while in Brazil many citizens practice African religions right along with Catholicism and Protestantism.

South America is a lightly populated continent, having just 6 percent of the world's people. It is also the world's most tropical continent, for a larger percentage of its land falls between the tropics of Cancer and Capricorn than is the case with any other continent. The world's driest desert is there, the Atacama in northern Chile, where no one has ever seen a drop of rain fall. And the world's wettest place is there too, the Chocó region of Colombia, along that country's border with Panama. There it rains almost every day. South America also has some of the world's highest mountains, the Andes,

A bull and bullfighter face off in the ring at the Plaza de Toros, Bogotá.

and its greatest river, the Amazon.

So welcome to South America! Through this colorfully illustrated series of books you will travel through 12 countries, from giant Brazil to small Suriname. On your way you will learn about the geography, the history, the economy, and the people of each one. Geared to the needs of teachers and students, each volume contains book and web sources for further study, a chronology, project and report ideas, and even recipes of tasty and easy-to-prepare dishes popular in the countries studied. Each volume describes the country's national holidays and the cities and towns where they are held. And each book is indexed.

You are embarking on a voyage of discovery that will take you to lands not so far away, but as interesting and exotic as any in the world.

Colombia, the fourth-largest country in South America, is a land of great geographic contrasts. (Opposite) Tequendama Falls, near Bogotá, is a popular tourist attraction. The falls plunge more than 400 feet (1,312 meters) into the Andean jungle. (Right) Evening falls over Pasto, in the shadow of Galeras volcano.

1 Land of Contrasts

¡HOLA! ARE YOU discovering Colombia? It's a land of extremes, where one can climb towering, snowy mountains, stretch out on sunny tropical beaches, explore steamy *rain forest* jungles, and hike through a dry desert—all without leaving the country.

Gateway to South America

Located on the northwestern edge of South America, Colombia borders two great bodies of water. To the northeast lies the blue Caribbean Sea, and to the northwest the calm Pacific Ocean. Colombia also shares borders with Panama to the northwest, Venezuela to the east, Brazil to the southeast, Peru to the south, and Ecuador to the southwest. Its territory includes two small offshore islands in the Pacific and several island groups in the Caribbean.

The diverse terrain of Colombia covers 439,733 square miles (1,138,910 square kilometers), which is slightly more land area than the states of California and Texas combined. The fourth-largest country in South America, Colombia is smaller than only Brazil, Argentina, and Peru.

Because of its border with the **Isthmus** of Panama, Colombia is often referred to as the gateway to South America. To reach South America, early Indian tribes traveled southward through Colombia. The newcomers encountered spectacular scenery in a rugged land of many contrasts—highlands and lowlands, rain forests and desert land.

Highlands and Lowlands

The Andes mountain range, which divides the western portion of South America from south to north, splits into three distinct chains when it reaches Colombia. These high mountain ranges, or *cordilleras*, and deep river valleys make up the western third of the country—the Cordillera Occidental (western), the Cordillera Central (middle), and the Cordillera Oriental (eastern). Between the Oriental and Central mountain ranges runs the Magdalena River, Colombia's largest waterway at 956 miles (1,538 kilometers) long, while the Cauca River cuts a valley between the Central and Occidental.

The Cordillera Central and Oriental feature towering mountain peaks— the Nevada del Huila in the Cordillera Central reaches 18,865 feet (about 5,750 meters) above sea level. But the Sierra Nevada de Santa Marta—a separate range in the northeast that looms high over the Caribbean coast—contains Colombia's highest peak: the 18,947-foot (5,775-meter) Cristóbal Colón, named for the explorer Christopher Columbus.

Quick Facts: The Geography of Colombia

Location: northern South America, bordering both the Caribbean Sea and the Pacific Ocean, between Panama and Venezuela to the north and between Ecuador and Panama to the south

Area: (slightly more than the states of California and Texas combined)
total: 439,733 square miles (1,138,910 sq. km)
land: 401,042 square miles (1,038,700 sq. km)
water: 38,691 square miles (100,210 sq. km)

Borders: Brazil, 1,021 miles (1,643 km); Ecuador, 367 miles (590 km); Panama, 140 miles (225 km); Peru (est.), 930 miles (1,496 km); Venezuela, 1,274 miles (2,050 km)

Climate: varies from hot in lowland plains to the east; steamy and tropical in rain forests in south and along coasts; cooler in mountain plateaus at higher elevations. The dry season runs from December to February, while the rainy season varies.

Terrain: coastal seashore, plains, and high mountains

Elevation extremes:
lowest point: Pacific Ocean, Caribbean Sea—0 feet
highest point: Pico Cristóbal Colón—18,947 feet (5,775 meters)

Natural hazards: occasional volcanic eruptions in the highlands, occasional earthquakes, droughts

Source: Adapted from the CIA World Factbook, 2001.

Most of Colombia's people live in the mountains—along the plateaus, valleys, and basins of the Andes. In prehistoric times ash from volcanic peaks created a fertile farmland in valleys lying between the three cordilleras. Sometimes volcanic eruptions create great destruction, though. In 1985 seismic activity of Nevado del Ruiz, located in the Cordillera Central, led to an ice and mudslide that buried most of the town of Armero in the valley below, killing approximately 25,000 people.

Earthquakes have also devastated areas in the western half of Colombia. A 1983 quake destroyed many old buildings and churches in the historic city of Popayán; a 1999 earthquake in La Tebaida killed about 1,000 people and left 250,000 homeless.

In the east, north, and far west of Colombia, the high mountains give way to the lowlands of the country's seacoast and plains. The waves of the Caribbean and Pacific wash against nearly 2,000 miles (3,219 km) of shoreline. Busy seaports and open areas of sandy beaches, palm trees, and resort towns occupy much of the populous Caribbean coastline. Fewer people live along the Pacific's rainy and heavily forested seashore, where small beaches dot long rocky stretches of land.

A Colombian woman and her children walk past damage caused by an earthquake in Popayán in 1983.

A large area of Colombia's lowlands is composed of the *llanos*, or grassland plains, located east of the Andes. An enormous tract of open prairie, the llanos cover nearly a quarter of Colombia. They are part of South America's Orinoco Basin, named for the Orinoco River, which forms Colombia's eastern boundary with Venezuela.

Few crops can grow in the poor soil of the llanos, and most people who live on Colombia's plains raise cattle and horses. In this thinly populated and largely undeveloped frontier, travelers depend on dirt roads to get from place to place, although these usually become impassable during heavy rains and seasonal flooding. Most towns and villages are accessible by airplane or by boat, on the meandering river tributaries that lead to the Orinoco River.

Rain Forests and Deserts

South of the llanos lie the humid jungles of the Amazon Basin, the world's largest tropical rain forest. The Amazon River itself borders Colombia for only about 50 miles (80 km) in the extreme southeastern corner of the country. However, its rain forest and tributaries cover much of the country's southern region. Several national parks in the region shelter an enormous diversity of plants and animals.

Another thick, tropical rain forest lies in Colombia's northwest. Located near the border with Panama, in the remote Chocó region, this sparsely populated area is one of the wettest places in the Americas, with an average rainfall of 394 inches (1,001 centimeters) per year.

Northeast of the Chocó, steamy jungles give way to extremely dry desert land at the northernmost tip of Colombia. Here the narrow Guajira Peninsula, named for the Indian tribe that inhabits the region, extends out into the Caribbean. An arid land rich in coal and salt deposits, the Guajira is the country's largest desert. But it is not as hot as the Maracaibo Basin in Norte de Santander. This region, near Colombia's eastern border with Venezuela, is known as the hottest place in South America.

A Range of Climates

Although the equator crosses through Colombia, most areas of the country do not have a tropical climate. The weather varies, changing from hot to cold as one travels from the lowlands to the highlands. Within a specific region the average temperature tends to remain the same year-round: there are no changes of the seasons.

At the lowest elevations, along the seacoast and in the eastern lowlands, the weather is tropical—hot and moist. The Caribbean coastal port of Barranquilla has an average year-round temperature of 82°F (28°C). Similarly, the lowland areas of the Amazon rain forest average about 80°F (27°C), along with 50 to 175 inches (127 to 445 cm) in yearly rainfall.

Temperatures become mild higher up in the mountains, at heights between 3,000 and 6,000 feet (approximately 900 and 1,800 meters) above sea level. Cooler temperatures prevail at higher altitudes such as the elevation of Colombia's capital city, Bogotá. It lies about 8,660 feet (2,640 meters) above sea level in the Cordillera Oriental, and has an average temperature of 58°F (14°C) year-round. On the highest peaks in the mountains, especially at altitudes higher than about 16,000 feet (4,880 meters), temperatures remain cold enough for snow to linger year-round.

There is no regular rainy season in Colombia. Each year most of the country has one or two periods of heavy rainfall, and one or two dry seasons with little or no rainfall. The driest times of year usually occur from December through February.

A Vast Variety of Wildlife

The forests, swamps, mountains, seas, deserts, and plains that comprise Colombia are home to a great variety of *flora* (plants) and *fauna* (animal life). Numerous species of orchids, mosses, vines, ferns, and grasses grow in humid jungles, while birds ranging in size from tiny hummingbirds to the huge Andean condor nest in the mountains. Endangered species, such as the spectacled bear, share the forested slopes of the Andes with more common animals, such as the *pudu* (Andean deer) and Andean fox.

Ten percent of the world's plant and animal species live in Colombia. This great *biodiversity* is protected in the nation's 46 nature reserves, including Los Katios National Park, in northwestern Colombia, and Amacayacu National Park, in the Amazon Basin.

Colombia has a long history of violence and unrest, as this pre-Columbian stone statue of a native warrior (opposite) indicates. (Right) Members of the Communist group FARC march during a parade in San Vicente del Caguán. Tens of thousands have been killed as various groups fought for power in Colombia during the past 30 years.

2 A History of Struggle

THE PEOPLE OF Colombia boast of living in Latin America's oldest democracy. But that proud claim veils a dark truth: Colombia's history is laden with almost continual strife, and ongoing violence threatens the stability of Colombian society today.

Pre-Columbian Era

The first people of Colombia probably arrived as early as 20,000 B.C., although few records of these early Amerindian (American Indian) cultures remain. Around 500 B.C. the Chibcha Indians settled in the high basins of the Cordillera Oriental of the Andes. Like the powerful Inca tribes of Peru, the Chibcha worshipped the sun and made human sacrifices. They constructed

17

large villages and lived in mud-covered houses built of cane. The Chibcha farmed the land, raising mostly corn and potatoes. Craftsmen fashioned implements of copper and gold, and Chibcha pottery included cups and jugs.

Other tribes also settled in the area. They included the Tairona, who built stone aqueducts and roads, and the Sinú, who engineered complicated drainage systems to grow crops in marshlands. The various groups lived peacefully, trading among themselves for hundreds of years.

That way of life changed dramatically at the end of the 15th century when one of Christopher Columbus's fellow explorers landed on the Caribbean coast. Alonso de Ojeda's reports of the precious metals and gems he found in the "New World" (the phrase Europeans used to describe the Americas) inspired others to journey there. Their arrival brought about drastic changes for the *indigenous* (native) people, and an end to what is now called the *pre-Columbian* era (the period of time before Christopher Columbus came to the Americas).

Soon Spanish invaders, known as *conquistadors*, or conquerors, learned of El Dorado (Spanish for "the gilded man"). Centuries earlier, the Chibchas held yearly rituals in which a chief was gilded, or covered in gold dust. Then, in an elaborate ceremony, El Dorado and his nobles floated on a raft laden with emeralds and gold to the middle of Lake Guatavita. There the chief bathed in the waters, washing off the gold while his men cast valuable offerings into the lake.

To the Spanish and other Europeans, the legend of El Dorado came to represent a whole kingdom of gold and precious gems. Whoever found it would become fabulously rich.

The New Granada Colony

By the early 1500s Spanish explorers were laying claim to the New World for Spain—and amassing riches to ship back home. While some conquistadors sought to discover the fabled kingdom of gold, other fortune-seekers seized treasures from conquered tribes or forced Indian slaves to dig in emerald and gold mines.

In 1525, Rodrigo de Bastidas founded the first permanent Spanish settlement in South America—Santa Marta, on the Caribbean coast of present-day Colombia. Eight years later the seaport of Cartagena was founded nearby. A fortified city, it held the accumulating riches bound for Spain.

In 1536, Gonzalo Jiménez de Quesada set out from the Caribbean coast along the Magdalena Valley in search of El Dorado in Colombia's interior. Within two years he had defeated the Chibcha and founded the city of Santa Fe de Bogotá. He named the new Spanish colony Nuevo Reino de Granada, or New Granada, after a region in Spain.

Along with their quest for gold, the European conquerors brought diseases that were new to South America. Illnesses like measles and influenza killed thousands of Native Americans. Many others perished from the brutal life of forced labor.

The Spanish soon turned to Africa as a source of labor. Slave markets in Cartagena offered thousands of kidnapped Africans for sale, most of whom were forced to work in the mines or on the sugarcane plantations that arose around the coastal Spanish settlements.

In 1717, the government of Spain combined New Granada with other conquered territories (including present-day Venezuela, Ecuador, and Panama). The Spanish called the newly created region the Viceroyalty of New Granada and established Bogotá as its capital.

Independence and Dissent

By the late 1700s, growing numbers of New Granada's mostly *mestizo* (mixed Spanish and Indian) population rejected Spanish rule. Starting around 1780 the royalist government had to suppress a series of uprisings.

On July 20, 1810, a legislative council in Bogotá, led by Antonio Nariño, officially proclaimed New Granada's independence. But it was not until nine arduous years later, on August 7, 1819, that Simón Bolívar and Francisco de Paula Santander joined

Simon Bolivar (1783—1830) helped free much of South America from Spanish rule in the early 19th century. After defeating the Spaniards in 1819, he organized Gran Colombia (this included the present-day states of Colombia, Ecuador, Panama, and Venezuela) and became its first president.

forces at the Battle of Boyacá in a crucial victory that liberated the territory of New Granada from Spain.

Bolívar, known as *El Libertador* (the Liberator), helped organize the country's new government as a democratic republic. Called Gran ("Great") Colombia, in honor of Christopher Columbus, the nation encompassed present-day Venezuela, Panama, and Ecuador, as well as Colombia. Bolívar served as the new country's first president, with Santander as vice president.

But more conflict followed. In 1830, Venezuela and Ecuador withdrew from Gran Colombia and became separate nations. And the rise of two fiercely opposed political parties—the Conservatives and the Liberals— destabilized the country's fledgling government. The Conservatives, who were supported by most of Colombia's wealthy landowners, believed that the nation should have a strong central government, limited voting rights, and strong Roman Catholic influence in political affairs. Members of the Liberal Party disagreed. They called for more powerful local rule, legislative changes that would help the poor, expansion of voting, and reduction of Roman Catholic influence in government.

In the decades that followed, frequent disagreements between factions of the Conservative and Liberal parties led to armed conflicts. Still, the country remained democratic, with political leaders from both parties assuming power through regular elections.

The Republic of Colombia

As the Conservatives and Liberals struggled for control of Colombia's government throughout the 1800s, new constitutions replaced old ones. In

1886, Conservative legislators approved a constitution that established a strong central government and renamed the nation the Republic of Colombia.

Violent conflicts and battles between the Conservatives and Liberals continued. An especially bloody civil war occurred between 1899 and 1902. It was later called the War of the Thousand Days, and it took the lives of more than 100,000 people.

In 1903 Panama revolted against Colombia and withdrew from the republic. The Colombian government had opposed granting the United States the rights to build a shipping waterway—a canal—across the Isthmus of Panama, thereby linking the Atlantic and Pacific Oceans. By preventing Colombian troops from reaching the rebels, the United States helped Panama break away from Colombia—and ensured that construction of the Panama Canal could proceed.

Animosity between the Liberal and Conservative parties lasted well into the 20th century. In 1948, the assassination of a Liberal Party politician in Bogotá sparked a new wave of particularly brutal civil strife. Nearly 200,000 Colombian citizens died during *La Violencia* (The Violence), which began with riots in Bogotá and other cities and later spread to the countryside.

A military coup in 1953 led by General Gustavo Rojas Pinilla calmed the fighting and established a short-lived dictatorship. Three years later, the general was ousted and the Liberal and Conservative parties agreed to join forces, creating a coalition (joint) government known as the National Front. The two parties agreed to share major political offices equally and alternate the presidency. This power-sharing arrangement lasted until 1974.

Colombia Today

The democratic government of Colombia is similar to that of the United States in that it has three branches of power: executive (a president and vice president), legislative (a 102-member Senate and a 165-member Chamber of Representatives), and judicial (with 28 justices on the Supreme Court, Colombia's highest court). The governors of each of Colombia's 32 *departamentos* (departments, or states) are elected by popular vote. The national capital is the city and district of Bogotá. In 1990 legislators approved a new constitution that addressed human rights and social security issues.

Many hoped the new constitution would help Colombia deal with several severe problems. Of major concern was the defeat of organizations that used *guerrilla* tactics

Colombian police guard packages of seized cocaine. Illegal drug traffic has been a major problem in Colombia for more than two decades.

After being elected president of Colombia in May 2002, Alvaro Uribe Vélez (left) visited U.S. president George W. Bush in Washington, D.C., to discuss human rights, the drug problem, and security concerns. During his campaign, Uribe had promised to resolve the problem of leftist guerrillas.

(unconventional warfare) in efforts to overthrow the government. The 1960s and 1970s had witnessed the rise of several groups, including the Communist FARC (Revolutionary Armed Forces of Colombia) and ELN (National Liberation Army), and the dissident M-19 guerrillas. Despite occasional cease-fire truces and peace talks, antigovernment terrorism has continued. In early 2002, both the FARC and the ELN increased their revolutionary activities, sabotaging an oil pipeline and bridges, hijacking a Colombian airliner, and kidnapping a presidential candidate, Ingrid Betancourt. The guerrillas continue to control large areas of Colombia's countryside.

During the early 1990s yet another guerrilla group formed, the *paramilitary* AUC (United Self-Defense Forces of Colombia). The AUC, which has links to wealthy landowners and to segments of Colombia's military, is dedicated to fighting the Communist FARC and ELN.

The Colombian government must also contend with the illegal drug trade. Huge quantities of narcotics, particularly cocaine and heroin, are grown in, processed in, or smuggled through Colombia. Much of it is destined for the United States. Since the 1980s, drug *cartels* (organizations of drug traffickers) based in major cities such as Medellín and Cali have carried out campaigns of intimidation and assassination to protect their illegal operations. Hundreds of Colombians who dared to oppose the cartels—journalists, police officers, judges, politicians, and ordinary citizens alike—have been brutally killed. The FARC and ELN have also increasingly financed their terrorist operations with money earned through the illegal drug trade.

With financial and military assistance from the United States, Colombian military forces have recently tried to cut off the profits that help make the drug cartels and the terrorists so powerful—spraying herbicides to kill opium poppy and coca crops, destroying laboratories where cocaine and heroin are made, and intercepting shipments of illegal drugs bound for the United States. In late 1999 the Colombian government announced "Plan Colombia," a $5.3 billion program (with $1.3 billion provided by the United States) to stabilize the country, combat the narcotics industry, and bring about peace in a land long troubled by deadly violence.

Colombia was the leading flower-exporting nation in the Americas and was second in the world, behind only the Netherlands. Large farms strategically located near the international airports of Bogotá and Medellín raise a wide variety of flowers. Medellín orchids have become world famous.

Other agricultural exports include meat, milk, and leather from cattle raised on the plains by cowboys known as *llaneros*. Fishing and shrimp farming are major livelihoods along the coast of the Pacific Ocean and Caribbean Sea.

Altogether agricultural products make up about 19 percent of the country's *gross domestic product (GDP)*. That is, farming, ranching, and fishing account for about one-fifth of the total value of all the goods and services that Colombia produces in a year. In 2000 Colombia's GDP of approximately $81.3 billion ranked 41st among the world's economies, according to World Bank statistics.

Growth Industries: Textile and Petroleum Exports

About one-quarter of Colombians work in factories or mining-related businesses. Industry provides about 26 percent of the nation's GDP.

Many Colombian manufacturing plants are based in or near the major cities of Bogotá, Medellín, and Cali, where small, privately owned factories produce textiles, clothing, and leather goods; process food and beverages; or manufacture oil, metal products, chemicals, or cement. The textile industry, developed in the early part of the 20th century, produces one of the nation's leading manufactured goods—colorful fabrics made of Colombian-grown cotton.

A machine operator in a textile factory. Textile production has become an important part of Colombia's economy.

Mines produce fuels needed by an energy-hungry planet. From massive deposits located in La Guajira and near Barranquilla, workers extract large quantities of coal, most to be sold overseas. Colombia is a major supplier, ranking fifth worldwide in coal exports. The country also ranks eighth among oil-exporting nations. The highly successful crude petroleum industry originated in the early 1920s and remains strong thanks to the 1991 discovery of large petroleum reserves in the eastern foothills of the Andes and in the llanos. Oil may soon surpass coffee as Colombia's primary export. Colombia also has large reserves of natural gas and iron ore, as well as salt deposits, which provide material for the chemical industry.

The precious gems and metals that lured the Spanish to the area centuries earlier continue to bolster the country's economy. Emeralds are mined near Bogotá, and gold near Medellín. Today Colombia supplies more than 90 percent of the world's emeralds and is an important producer of platinum, gold, and silver.

Service Industries

About half of Colombia's people work in the service industry—at jobs in retail, banking, and insurance businesses, or in health, education, and government agencies. Service workers are cashiers and stockers, bank tellers

An airplane sprays herbicide on a poppy field in Huila (the poppy is used to produce heroin). Colombia is better known for production of cocaine: in 2000, it produced more than 500 metric tons of the drug, according to CIA estimates. About 90 percent of the cocaine that reaches the United States each year comes through Colombia.

Colombian workers manipulate equipment at the head of an oil rig in Cusiana. Colombia has become an important producer of oil.

and managers, sales representatives and office clerks. The service industry accounts for more than half of Colombia's GDP.

Workers are paid in pesos, Colombia's currency. One hundred centavos equals one peso. In early 2002, the rate of exchange was 2,353 Colombian pesos for 1 U.S. dollar.

Transportation and Energy

Because of the difficulties and high cost of constructing and maintaining railways in Colombia's rugged terrain, few railroads exist in the country. Major highways connect large cities to the north and south, but air travel remains the best form of transportation. International airports in Bogotá, Cali, Medellín, and Barranquilla handle much of Colombia's air traffic.

Hydroelectric plants located on rivers such as the Magdalena, Cauca, and Guavio provide most of Colombia's electrical power. Energy produced by coal provides the rest. The electricity distribution system is publicly owned.

Providing for the Future

Altogether 8.3 million people are employed in the labor force of Colombia. But the country suffers from a high unemployment rate: about 20 of every 100 workers have no job. The nation struggled with a severe recession in 1999, although growth in the oil industry helped prop up the economy.

Yet another problem has been Colombia's high *inflation* rate. Inflation refers to the increasing cost of goods and services in an economy over a period of time. If inflation remains high from year to year, everyday goods can become expensive and difficult for low-income workers to obtain. In Colombia, inflation was averaging more than 20 percent for several decades before falling into the single digits during the late 1990s.

Colombia has many poor people. A little more than half of its citizens live below the poverty line. Fewer than 3 percent of Colombians own an automobile. Some live in remote areas of the country that do not have electricity. The unequal distribution of wealth and opportunities among Colombia's citizens has contributed to civil unrest.

Colombia's efforts to sustain a healthy, stable economy have been helped by strong trade partnerships with the United States, Venezuela, Japan, and Germany. As a member of the Andean Common Market, Colombia also participates in trade with many of its South American neighbors. Colombia *imports* goods such as chemicals, machinery, and transportation equipment from abroad.

(Opposite) The ornate interior of a Roman Catholic cathedral in Bogotá. Most of Colombia's population is Catholic. (Right) Musicians at the Vallenato Festival in Valledupar. The people of Colombia celebrate numerous holidays, both religious and secular.

4 The Many Faces of Colombia's People

WITH ABOUT 41 million residents, Colombia ranks second in population of all South American countries. The nation contains a rich ethnic mixture, with its people claiming ancestry from three different continents: South America, Europe, and Africa. Most citizens are of mixed descent: more than half are *mestizos* (of Indian and white origin), one-fifth are *mulattoes* (mixed black and white), and a small fraction are *zambos* (mixed black and Indian). Another fifth of the population is white, or Creole (of European descent).

The country's official language, Spanish, unites this racial and cultural blend of peoples. However, some 400,000 Amerindians from 60 different ethnic groups speak both Spanish and their native tongues.

Guambiano Indians prepare their land for planting. The Guambianos are a tribe indigenous to Colombia; they live in the Andean highlands.

Religion and Education

Religious beliefs also unite the diverse people of Colombia. Nearly 95 percent of the country follows the Roman Catholic faith. Of the remaining 5 percent, some practice traditional native religions; others have joined growing Protestant sects, such as Jehovah's Witness, Mormon, Calvinist, and Lutheran.

About 9 of 10 Colombians over the age of 15 can read and write. This high literacy rate can be attributed to the government requirement that children attend school for at least five years. Children in rural areas tend to have less education because they do not have easy access to schools and because they are often kept home to work on family farms. Colombia has about 40 universities, most located in major cities. The largest is the Universidad Nacional, located in Bogotá.

Quick Facts: The People of Colombia

Population: 41,008,227

Ethnic groups: mestizo, 58%; white (European, chiefly Spanish), 20%; mixed black-white, 14%; black, 4%; mixed black—Native American, 3%; Native American, 1%

Age structure:
0—14 years: 31.6%
15—64 years: 63.6%
65 years and over: 4.8%

Population growth rate: 1.6%

Birth rate: 21.99 births/1,000 population

Death rate: 5.66 deaths/1,000 population

Infant mortality rate: 23.21 deaths/1,000 live births

Life expectancy at birth:
total population: 70.85 years
male: 67 years
female: 74.83 years

Total fertility rate: 2.64 children born per woman

Religions: Roman Catholic, 95%; Evangelical Protestant, approximately 4%

Languages: Spanish (official), various Amerindian languages

Literacy rate (age 15 and older): 91.3% (1995 est.)

All figures are 2002 estimates unless otherwise noted.
Source: CIA World Factbook, 2002.

Food, Drink, and Clothing

In Colombia the biggest meal is eaten at midday and usually consists of soup, a main course, and a drink. Main courses may include starchy foods such as potatoes, rice, and cassava root, as well as a meat such as chicken, pork, or beef. Fruit juices and soft drinks are common beverages, although many people savor a cup of hot sugarcane water, known as *agua de panela*, with their food. Hot chocolate is also popular.

Some cities have regional specialties. In Bogotá, a hearty chicken and potato stew known as *ajiaco* satisfies many an appetite. The state of Tolima offers *lechona*, a roasted suckling pig stuffed with rice. *Bandeja paisa*, a meat dish accompanied by cassava, rice, fried plantain, and red beans, is served in the Medellín area. *Arepas*, or corn pancakes, are a popular breakfast dish throughout Colombia. Meals may include a variety of Colombia's locally grown tropical fruits, including exotic ones such as *maracuyá* and *curuba*.

Most urban middle- and upper-class Colombians wear the same style of clothing as people in the United States and Europe. In rural areas, some prefer more traditional garb, such as the *ruana*, a plain woolen cloak.

Sports and Festivals

Children and adults alike consider soccer (called *fútbol* in Spanish-speaking countries) their favorite sport, both to play and to watch. Victories in international tournaments such as the *Copa America* (Americas Cup), the oldest Latin American soccer competition, produce particularly spirited displays of nationalistic fever. With a hard-fought win comes great rejoicing

A woman places *arepas* (corn pancakes) on a hot grill.

in the streets, as enthusiastic fans honk horns, cheer, and wave flags in passionate celebration.

Many major cities, such as Bogotá, Cali, Medellín, Manizales, and Cartagena, feature modern sports facilities and arenas for two other popular sports—boxing and bullfighting. Spanish colonists brought bullfighting with them to South America; a yearly fair in Manizales attracts many fans. Even American baseball, mostly played in the port cities of Cartagena and Barranquilla, draws a crowd.

Colombians enjoy 18 official national holidays, 12 of which are Christian celebrations. Cities across the nation celebrate *Carnaval*, held just before the beginning of Lent, with colorful parades, floats, and dances. The most

Colombia's national *fútbol* (soccer) team poses for a picture before a game against rival Bolivia. Many Colombians are passionate about *fútbol*.

famous Carnaval festivities take place in Barranquilla. Tourists flock to the provincial city of Popayán, located in southwestern Colombia, during *Semana Santa*, or Holy Week, for its renowned Easter celebrations.

Nonreligious holidays may honor historical events, such as Independence Day (July 20), which recalls Colombia's first official proclamation of independence from Spain. Local celebrations such as the flower festival in Medellín or sugarcane festival in Cali celebrate a region's major product.

Arts, Music, and Literature

Pre-Columbian Indians produced impressive works of art, although most of their intricate gold and silver metalwork was destroyed, melted into ingots by Spanish conquistadors. Bogotá's Gold Museum contains about 35,000 gold items that survived, including jewelry, musical instruments, bowls, and even a miniature model of El Dorado's legendary raft.

A Colombian man weaves a mat by hand in San Martín. Many artisans still use traditional methods to create baskets, pottery, and other items.

A crowd near the Emerald Street market in Bogotá.

The past also still lives in the stone sculptures and pottery found in many archaeological sites, including San Agustín, located to the southwest of Bogotá. There, hundreds of huge stone-carved figures, some more than 5,000 years old, portray the gods and mythical animals of a long-extinct culture. The nearby site of Tierradentro features ancient burial chambers and decorated tombs carved out of rock.

Colombian artisans today often mingle Native American, Spanish, and African traditions in their handicrafts, using distinctive patterns, designs, or techniques in basketry, embroidery, textile weaving, and pottery.

Similarly, Colombian music and dance reflect a blending of cultures as well. African rhythms and Caribbean sounds combine in two of Colombia's best-known musical genres: the *cumbia* and the *vallenato*. The members of a *cumbia* band play *gaitas* (flutes) and drums, while an accordion, *caja* drums (similar to a bongo), and a *guacharaca* (a bamboo cane played with a small metallic fork) provide the *vallenato* sound. Cities around the country host annual folk dance and music competitions of the *cumbia*, *vallenato*, and their variants. Other native music instruments are the *tiple* (a small, 12-string guitar) and the maraca (a rattle made from a gourd).

The best-known Colombian writer is novelist Gabriel García Márquez (1928–   ). His works, many of which are based on the history and culture of his country, are considered among the finest of Latin American literature. His best-known novel is *Cien años de soledad* (One Hundred Years of Solitude), which has been translated into more than 30 languages. García Márquez's works received special honor in 1982 when he was awarded the Nobel Prize in literature.

(Opposite) High-rise office buildings and apartments look down on a bull-ring in the center of Bogotá. (Right) The influence of the Spaniards who established Cartagena in the early 16th century is evident in the architecture of these buildings along Calle San Pedro Claver. Cartagena remains one of Colombia's most important seaports.

5 A Progressively More Urban Society

MORE THAN 70 percent of the people of Colombia live in just 10 of its cities, either in the mountains or along the Caribbean coast. Since the 1940s more and more Colombians have moved from rural farms to urban regions, where many have established comfortable lifestyles, with easy access to shops, schools, and medical care. However, poor, uneducated city dwellers, many of them children, struggle to survive in the streets and shantytowns that have sprung up around the booming cities.

The Major Industrial Centers

The population of **Bogotá**, Colombia's largest city, skyrocketed from 660,000 in 1951 to more than 7 million in 2000. Currently the 20th most dense-ly inhabited city in the world, Bogotá contains thriving factories and businesses, elegant theaters, fancy restaurants, state-of-the-art sports facilities, and a modern public transit system.

Located in a high valley of the Cordillera Oriental, Bogotá was originally settled by the Chibcha Indians, who called the area "Bacatá." Renamed Santa Fe de Bogotá in 1538 by conquering Spaniards, the town began to flourish in 1900 after a railway linked it to the Magdalena River. The narrow streets and historic squares of its colonial days have been preserved in La Candelaria, a popular tourist attraction located in the heart of the cosmopolitan city.

A busy industrial center, Bogotá produces about one-third of Colombia's manufactured goods. These include pharmaceutical products, processed foods and beverages, clothing, books, tires, and automobiles.

Villa de Leyva was the center of government when the Republic of New Granada declared its independence from Spain in 1810; today, this attractive town is considered a national monument.

From this hill pedestrians can look over the town of Pasto. The Galeras volcano looms over the town in southern Colombia, which was founded by Spaniards in the mid-16th century.

Second in size to Bogotá is **Cali**, located in the south of Colombia, on the eastern slope of the Cordillera Occidental in the Cauca Valley. Sometimes referred to as the southern capital of Colombia, the vibrant industrial city of Cali claims a population of more than 1.7 million. Its major industries include paper and chemical manufacturing; surrounding farms produce sugarcane and rice. Because it is located at a lower altitude than Bogotá (3,378 feet, or 1,030 meters), Cali has a mild, spring-like climate year-round.

Founded in 1536 by Spanish conquistador Sebastián de Belalcázar, Cali remained a sleepy colonial town until 1900, when the newly built railway connected it to the Pacific port city of Buenaventura. Tourists abandoned Cali beginning in the 1980s, when conflicts among drug cartels escalated to bombings, assassinations, and kidnappings.

Tile-roofed houses in the rural village of Monserrate.

Another city afflicted by drug-related violence is Colombia's third-largest metropolis, **Medellín** (population 1,621,356), the leading textile center in Latin America. Most residents try to carry on with business as usual in the industrial town, which produces more than 80 percent of the nation's textiles. Other plants in Medellín process food; make bricks; tan leather; or produce agricultural machinery, glass and china, paints, and chemicals.

Located in the Cordillera Central, at an altitude of 4,877 feet (1,487 meters), Medellín was founded in the 17th century. Fertile fields that surround the city generate much of Colombia's coffee, whose introduction in the 1800s spurred the city's growth. Industrialization followed in the early 1900s, with the arrival of the first weaving looms.

Major Seaports

Early settlers founded the busy port city of **Barranquilla** in 1629, a few miles inland from the Caribbean Sea, along the west bank of the Magdalena River. Today Barranquilla serves not only as a major seaport but also as a center for Colombia's textile industry. With a population of more than a million, Barranquilla is Colombia's fourth-largest city, and a popular stop with tourists wishing to visit colonial Spanish palaces and cathedrals, relax on scenic beaches, and attend the city's famous Carnaval celebrations.

Southwest of Barranquilla, on the Caribbean, lies the beach resort and colonial city of **Cartagena**. The Spanish explorer Pedro de Heredia founded the port in 1533 to store gold and silver for shipment to Spain. During the next two centuries, protective walls, or ramparts, and forts were built to defend the city from pirate attacks. Many of these fortifications remain today, and along with the city's colonial monasteries, plazas, and mansions, draw millions of visitors to Cartagena each year.

Today, as a major Caribbean seaport, Cartagena ships many of Colombia's exports, including coffee, leather products, alligator skins, cattle, hides, tobacco, textiles, and petroleum. A pipeline runs from inland oil fields to the city's harbor and refineries.

Further east on the Caribbean coastline lies **Santa Marta**, the oldest permanent Spanish settlement in South America. Today, the city is Colombia's smallest Caribbean port, and bananas are its principal export. Visitors to Santa Marta usually journey to the nearby archaeological site of Ciudad Perdida (Lost City). Discovered in 1975, these ancient stone ruins were the cultural center of the Tairona Indian tribe, one of the most advanced early civilizations of Colombia.

Colombia's leading seaport on the Pacific coast is **Buenaventura** (population: 193,185). Founded in 1540, the city is best known for its exports of coffee, bananas, gold, hides, platinum, and sugar.

A Calendar of Colombian Festivals

With its Roman Catholic majority, Colombia celebrates many religious as well as historical holidays. Individual towns may also honor their patron saints or celebrate local events. Most Colombian festivals feature processions and parades, dancing, food, and fun.

JANUARY

New Year's celebrations run from Christmas to January 6, or **Epiphany**. In Cali, festivities include bullfights, horse parades, masked balls, sporting events, and salsa competitions.

In early January, the people of Pasto celebrate the **Carnaval de Blancos y Negros** (Festival of Whites and Blacks). On January 5, or Día de los Negros (Black Day), people try to mark one another with black grease or shoe polish. The following day, Día de los Blancos, or White Day, they throw talc or flour.

The **Feria de Manizales**, or Manizales Fair, takes place in early January, complete with bullfights, beauty parades, and folk dancing. Bogotá hosts its own bullfighting fair, **Temporada Taurina**, the same month.

FEBRUARY

On February 2 citizens of Cartagena celebrate **La Candelaria** (Candlemas). The feast day is preceded by a candlelight procession up La Popa hill to the Augustinian church. Its statue of the Virgin of La Candelaria is said to protect believers from plague and pirates.

The four-day **Carnaval de Barranquilla** (Barranquilla Carnival), which leads up to Lent, features parades with floats, masked and costumed performers, dancing, beauty contests, and a two-day music festival.

MARCH

Early in the month a weeklong international film festival takes place in Cartagena. The **Festival Internacional de Cine de Cartagena** features recent Colombian, Latin American, and Ibero-American films.

APRIL

Semana Santa, or Holy Week, may fall in March or April. Celebrations take place throughout the country as part of Easter Week, including Holy Thursday, Good Friday, and Easter Sunday. Many cities host religious processions, with the most famous celebrations taking place in Popayán, Mompox, and Pamplona.

Thousands attend the annual folk music competition and festival held during the end of the month in Valledupar. It is called the F**estival de la Leyenda Vallenata**.

MAY

May 1 is **Labor Day** in Colombia.

Religious holidays celebrated in May include **Ascension Day, Corpus Christi**, and the **Feast of the Sacred Heart**.

JUNE

June festivals that celebrate central Colombian

folk dances and music include the **Fiesta del Bambuco**, held in Neiva, and the **Festival Folklórico Colombiano**, held in Ibagué toward the end of the month. Festivals based on music originating from the Caribbean coast include the **Festival de la Cumbia** in El Banco, and the **Festival del Porro** in San Pelayo.

JULY

On July 20, Colombians celebrate their **Independence Day**, marking the day in 1810 when a legislative council in Bogotá proclaimed New Granada's independence from Spain.

Residents of Santa Marta celebrate their city's founding with parades and musical performances during the **Festival Patronal de Santa Marta**.

AUGUST

On August 7, Colombians remember the **Battle of Boyacá**, Simón Bolívar's decisive victory over the Spanish in 1819, which ensured Colombia's independence.

August 15 is the **Assumption of the Virgin Mary**, an important Catholic feast day.

Medellín's **Feria de las Flores y Desfile de Silleteros** (Flower Fair and Parade of the Flower Vendors) is a several-day celebration held during the first half of August. It includes one of the most spectacular parades in Colombia, an immensely popular tourist attraction.

SEPTEMBER

Described as the Latin American equivalent of Saint Valentine's Day, **Amor y Amistad** is celebrated for a week in Medellín.

OCTOBER

October 12, **Columbus Day**, commemorates the discovery of the Americas by the Italian-born explorer for whom Colombia is named.

NOVEMBER

November 1 is the Catholic holiday **All Saints' Day**.

The **Independence of Cartagena**, or **Independencia**, is celebrated on November 11. Though it is a national holiday, Independencia receives special attention in Cartagena. Dressed in masks and fancy costumes, revelers dance in the streets to lively Caribbean music; other festivities include beauty contests and battles of flowers.

DECEMBER

The **Immaculate Conception**, a Catholic feast day celebrating the freedom from original sin of Mary, the mother of Jesus, is celebrated on December 8.

Another important Christian holiday, **Christmas**, commemorates Jesus' birth and is celebrated December 25.

On New Year's Eve, December 31, Pasto and Ipiales mark the beginning of the new year by doing away with the old. That night is the **Concurso de Años Viejos**, when large dolls representing people or events of the past year are burned.

51

Recipes

Sancocho de Gallina (Chicken Soup)

chicken stock (1 1/2 quarts)
1 cassava, peeled and cut into 1-inch cubes
2 plantains, peeled, halved, and sliced into thirds longitudinally
2 red potatoes, peeling optional, cut into chunks
3 whole chicken breasts, skinned and quartered with bones left on
Juice from 2 lemons
1 tsp cumin
1 bunch scallions
1 bunch cilantro
Roux (2 tbs all-purpose flour and 2 tbs butter, mixed and microwaved for 30 seconds)
Salt and pepper

Directions:

1. In one cup of chicken stock, simmer scallions, cilantro, and cumin for a few minutes. Let cool, then process the mixture in a blender.
2. In the remaining 1 1/4 quarts of chicken stock, simmer the quartered, skinned chicken breasts for about one hour. Skim off and discard fat that floats to the surface.
3. As the chicken starts to simmer, add cassava and potatoes.
4. About a half hour from completion time, add plantains.
5. Ten minutes before completion time, add the processed mixture of scallions, cilantro, and cumin, and the lemon juice.
6. Add roux to "bind" the soup, stirring to mix it well. Add salt and pepper to taste.

Arepas (Cornmeal Pancakes)

Corn on the cob
Salt
Cornstarch

Directions:

1. Remove the corn from the cob and grind in a blender (don't use canned corn).
2. Add some salt, and some cornstarch to reduce the watery consistency.
3. Knead dough until it forms a firm ball, then form into several round, flat tortillas.
4. Prepare as you would cook pancakes on a pan. Serve hot with butter, salt, and white cheese.

Patacones (Fried Plantains)

4 large green plantains
Vegetable oil
Salt

Directions:
1. Peel the plantains and cut into 3 or 4 pieces.
2. Fry the pieces in hot vegetable oil.
3. When golden, take them out of the oil and pound them flat.
4. Return them to the oil and refry for a few minutes. Remove and place on absorbent paper towels. Sprinkle salt to taste.

Arepas de Chocolo (Fresh Corn Tortillas)

Corn on the cob
Salt
Cornstarch

Directions:
1. Remove the corn from the cob and grind in a blender (don't use canned corn).
2. Add some salt, and some cornstarch to reduce the watery consistency.
3. Knead dough until it forms a firm ball, then form into several round, flat tortillas.
4. Prepare as you would cook pancakes on a pan. Serve hot with butter, salt, and white cheese.

Carne en Polvo (Ground Beef)

1 lb beef, cut in chunks
Garlic and onion
Salt
5 tbs oil
2 onions, finely chopped
2 small tomatoes, chopped
1 cup water

Directions:
1. Marinate the meat overnight with garlic, onion, and salt.
2. Fry the beef, along with the onions, scallions, and tomatoes, in hot oil in a covered frying pan.
3. Add water and stir to make a sauce. Replace the cover and cook the meat for another five minutes.
4. Remove the pieces of beef and process in a meat grinder.
5. Add the ground meat mixture to the sauce. Blend thoroughly.
6. Serve hot with beans and rice.

Glossary

biodiversity—biological variety, as measured by the numbers of different species of plants and animals.

cartel—a loose organization of independent businesses in a particular field, whose goals are to fix prices and limit competition.

conquistador—a leader in the Spanish conquest of Central and South America.

cordillera—a long chain of mountains or mountain ranges.

departamentos—departments, or states; Colombia has 32 *departamentos* and one capital district.

exports—goods that are sold outside the country of origin.

fauna—the animal life of a particular region.

flora—the plants and vegetation of a particular region.

gross domestic product (GDP)—the total value of all the goods and services produced in a country annually.

guerrilla—a person who carries out warfare in an unconventional way, including sabotage, kidnapping, and assassination.

imports—goods that are brought into a country from another land for use or sale there.

indigenous—native or original to a particular area.

inflation—the increasing cost of goods and services in an economy over a period of time.

isthmus—a narrow strip of land connecting two larger land areas.

llanos—grassland plains of Spanish America.

llaneros—cowboys who herd cattle on the plains.

mestizo—a person of mixed Spanish and Indian heritage.

mulatto—a person of mixed African and European heritage.

paramilitary—relating to military forces that do not form part of a country's regular armed forces, but that are often supported or tolerated by the government or regular army.

pre-Columbian—the period of time in the Americas before the arrival of Christopher Columbus.

rain forest—a wooded area with annual rainfall of at least 100 inches (254 centimeters).

zambo—a person of mixed African and Indian heritage.

Project and Report Ideas

Journal Writing

Choose a colonial city (such as Bogotá, Cartagena, or Popayán) or archaeological site (San Agustín, Tierradentro, Ciudad Perdida) in Colombia that you would like to learn more about. Research the site, recording important facts on index cards. Then write a fictional journal entry about a visit to that site. Journals should include vivid descriptions and be written in the first person, from the point of view of a tourist.

Poster or Brochure

Create a poster or brochure advertising one of the following geographic regions of Colombia: the Andes, the seacoast, the llanos, or the rain forest. Find at least four images from travel magazines or from Internet searches that illustrate the area and include them in your advertisement, along with explanatory captions.

Create an Export Map

Using a key to represent various products, create a map that answers these questions:
- Where are the following agricultural products raised: coffee, cut flowers, bananas, rice, tobacco, corn, sugarcane, cocoa beans; cattle; shrimp?
- Where are some of the following reserves and industries located: petroleum, natural gas, coal, iron ore, nickel, gold, copper, emeralds?
- Where are Colombia's major industrial areas, agricultural regions, and seaports?

Reports

Write one-page biographies on any of the following people:
- Simón Bolívar
- Antonio Nariño
- Christopher Columbus
- Gonzalo Jiménez de Quesada
- Francisco de Paula Santander

Project and Report Ideas

Choose one of the following topics and write a one-page report describing its history, including dates of significant events:

- Building the Panama Canal
- The Colombian coffee industry
- Conquest of the Chibcha Indians
- The Copa America soccer tournament
- Major advances of the Tairona Indian people
- Colombia's most destructive volcanoes

Geography Map

Create a map of Colombia that includes the following features:

- Pacific Ocean, Caribbean Sea
- Surrounding countries of Panama, Venezuela, Brazil, Peru, and Ecuador
- Major rivers, including the Amazon, Orinoco, Magdalena, and Cauca
- Area of greatest rainfall
- Area of least rainfall
- Area with very high temperatures
- Area with very low temperatures
- San Andrés Island, Guajira Peninsula, Cristóbal Colón, Chaco and Amazon rain forests, the llanos grasslands

Chronology

ca. 500 B.C.	Chibcha Indian tribes settle in the central highlands of Colombia.
early 1500s	Spanish explorers make their way to present-day Colombia and claim it for Spain.
1525	Rodrigo de Bastidas founds Santa Marta, South America's first permanent Spanish settlement.
1538	Gonzalo Jiménez de Quesada defeats the Chibcha, and names the conquered territory New Granada; founds the town of Bogotá.
1717	Spain creates the Viceroyalty of New Granada, which includes present-day Colombia, Venezuela, Ecuador, and Panama.
1810	Citizens in Bogotá rebel against Spanish rule, proclaiming an official Act of Independence on July 20.
1819	Venezuelan general Simón Bolívar defeats Spanish royalists at Boyacá on August 7; Bolívar unites Colombia, Venezuela, Panama, and Ecuador as Gran Colombia.
1830	Venezuela and Ecuador break away from Gran Colombia; factions of Liberal and Conservative parties engage in armed conflicts throughout the rest of the century.
1886	New constitution establishes the Republic of Colombia.
1899–1903	War of a Thousand Days.
1903	Panama withdraws from Gran Colombia.
1948	Beginning of *La Violencia* (The Violence), a civil war that results in the deaths of about 200,000.

Chronology

1957	Liberal and Conservative politicians join together to create the National Front.
1960s–1970s	Guerrilla groups organize to oppose policies of the government.
1970s–1980s	Colombia becomes international center for illegal drug trade; with support of the United States, Colombian government begins effort to end drug trafficking within its borders.
1991	New national constitution becomes valid July 5.
2000	U.S. government votes money to support "Plan Colombia," a program devised by Colombian president Andrés Pastrana whose goals include fighting drug traffickers and rebel groups.
2002	Peace talks between the government and the guerrilla group FARC break down; Alvaro Uribe is elected president on a platform of making the country safe from guerrilla violence.
2003	A referendum seeking support for President Uribe's political reforms is voted down.
2004	The government offers a prisoner exchange program with FARC and ELN, in an attempt to negotiate to end the civil war.

Further Reading/Internet Resources

Cameron, Sara J. *Out of War: True Stories from the Front Lines of the Children's Movement for Peace in Colombia.* New York: Scholastic Press, 2001.

Henderson, James D. *Modernization in Colombia: The Laureano Gómez Years.* Gainesville: Florida University Press, 2001.

Pollard, Peter. *Colombia Handbook: The Travel Guide.* Chicago: Footprint Handbooks Books, 2000.

Vega, Pablo Corral. "In the Shadow of the Andes." *National Geographic*, Feb. 2001.

History and Geography

http://www.lonelyplanet.com/destinations/south_america/colombia/
http://lcweb2.loc.gov/frd/cs/cotoc.html
http://www.infoplease.com/countryprofilenotes.html

Economic and Political Information

http://www.state.gov/r/pa/ei/bgn/35754.htm
http://www.odci.gov/cia/publications/factbook/geos/co.html
http://www.colostate.edu/Orgs/LASO/Colombia/colombia.html

The official promotion and regulating agency for tourism is the Dirección General de Turismo, which can be reached at the following address:

Dirección General de Turismo
Ministerio de Desarrollo Económico
Calle 28, No. 13a - 15, Piso 17
Santa Fé de Bogotá
Colombia
Telephone: +57 1 352 2105
Email: turismo@mindesa.gov.co

Additional information is available at the Embassy of Colombia, located in the United States at the following address:

**Embassy of Colombia
to the United States**
2118 Leroy Pl., NW
Washington, DC 20008
Phone: 202-387-8338
Fax: 202-232-8643
Email: emwas@colombiaemb.org
Website: http://www.colombiaemb.org/

**U.S. Department of Commerce
Trade Information Center**
International Trade Administration
14th and Constitution Ave., NW
Washington, DC 20230
Telephone: 800-USA-TRADE
Website: http://www.ita.doc.gov

Index

Index/Picture Credits

Contributors

Senior Consulting Editor **James D. Henderson** is professor of international studies at Coastal Carolina University. He is the author of *Conservative Thought in Twentieth Century Latin America: The Ideals of Laureano Gómez* (1988; Spanish edition *Las ideas de Laureano Gómez* published in 1985); *When Colombia Bled: A History of the Violence in Tolima* (1985; Spanish edition *Cuando Colombia se desangró, una historia de la Violencia en metrópoli y provincia*, 1984); and co-author of *A Reference Guide to Latin American History* (2000) and *Ten Notable Women of Latin America* (1978).

   Mr. Henderson earned a bachelor's degree in history from Centenary College of Louisiana, and a master's degree in history from the University of Arizona. He then spent three years in the Peace Corps, serving in Colombia, before earning his doctorate in Latin American history in 1972 at Texas Christian University.

LeeAnne Gelletly is a freelance writer and editor living outside Philadelphia, Pennsylvania. She has worked in publishing for more than 20 years.